THE MARK
OF THE
BEAST
Is Already in Your Hand
Your Eyes See It without Seeing It

KENNETH LEE SPEARS

ISBN 978-1-63903-575-5 (paperback)
ISBN 978-1-63903-576-2 (digital)

Christian Faith Publishing, Inc.
832 Park Avenue
Meadville, PA 16335
www.christianfaithpublishing.com

Printed in the United States of America

Contents

Introduction...5
Chart 7

Chapter 1:   Origin of the Mark of the Beast................................9
Chapter 2:   Mark in the Right Hand 13
Chapter 3:   Mark in the Forehead...18
Chapter 4:   The Temple..27

INTRODUCTION

The mark of the beast is already here!
Hidden in plain sight!

Understand that if there is something as huge and as widely studied as the mark of the beast, it would be very difficult to hide. But realize it is a well-known concept that many times, the best place to hide things is in plain sight. This book will reveal that this is exactly what was done and why the Bible teaches your eyes will see without seeing (Matthew 13:13).

U se this chart to help follow the context and see how it's all related and falls into place in these times as I have now proven. If the Pleiades and Apollyon are clearly mentioned in the Bible and Apollyon's son, Asclepius, can be traced as the son of Perdition (also mentioned in the Bible), then obviously, all their other children, Nephilim, would exist as well. This chart shows all these fallen ones (demons, the Nephilim) that are at work in these times.

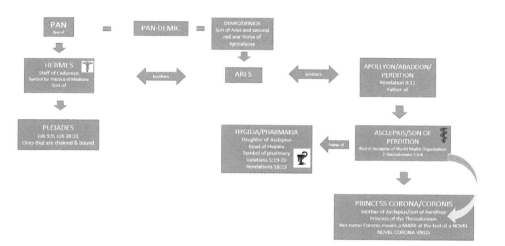

CHAPTER 1

ORIGIN OF THE MARK
OF THE BEAST

I would like to begin by pointing out what I believe is one of the most important verses in Scripture that reveals what God is: John 1:1. God is the Word. In knowing this, try to discern that we are made in his image as Scripture states. If you consider this concept and compile it with Isaiah 46:9, "remember the ancient things," and apply them together conceptually as a whole, one might be able to conclude that through our discernment of the world, we should be able to determine what exactly the mark of the beast in the right hand is in line with the scripture Revelation 13:18.

Over the centuries, there have been much speculation, stipulation, and many attempts to determine what this mark is. In many cases, it falls very short of a complete application as alluded to in Scripture. It lacks elements of fullness as described in Scripture. In this book, I intend to show and prove unequivocally that I alone have knowledge of the mark of the beast and that I can prove it in complete alignment with Scripture like no one ever has. Also, I will reveal that we are currently in the times that this mark will be implemented.

To understand the mark completely, you must first learn its origins. There was what we call research and development that also allowed this mark to become slowly implemented and accepted by mankind. We as consumers are driven by the supply-and-demand nature of our personalities. We always want better, easier lifestyles; hence, new tech devices are always being developed. Also, innovation companies take our desires and create new devices that we end up making part of our daily lives to a point we believe we cannot live without them and even to a point of idolatry, which is expressly warned of in Scripture. Considering this and being that Lucifer is well aware of our human nature, he would obviously make the mark something we would not want to live without, making the mark widely accepted just as Scripture states.

I will begin with the origin of it all in 1902. A major tech breakthrough was invented called the "mercury-arc rectifier," invented by Peter Cooper Hewitt.

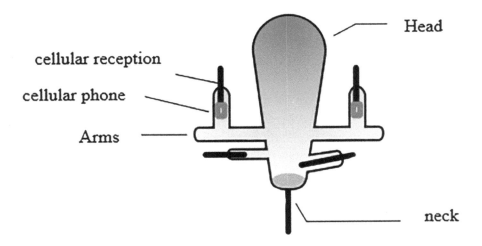

This was huge, but amazingly, it's not taught in schools. You have to wonder why. My opinion is this: it's Lucifer's crafty method to not publicize his means. This device was an AC/DC converter that revolutionized the times by converting alternating current into direct current. For those old enough to remember, AC/DC was, at a point, considered an acronym for "after Christ/devil's child" but has since been forgotten and discarded because as I've mentioned, people now love and rely on this for a better, more comfortable life-style, and it did not prove to be harmful. Let's be clear that I'm not saying this was the mark. This was merely a precursor to condition-ally program people to accept it. Realize that Lucifer has been here a long time and has been playing the long game. With that being said, understand that this was the beginning technology of many things including radio communication technology. This one device was the beginning development of what has now evolved into cellular phone technology.

I want to pause on the evolution of this device and give some deeper discernment. Look at its name first, "Mercury," which will be more relevant as it will relate to the mark in the head later in the book. Let's focus on the other two words. Notice *arc* is synonymously associated with the ark of the covenant in Scripture and, more impor-tantly, Noah's ark from the story of Genesis where God cleansed the earth of all the wickedness and giants/Nephilim to make things right again. Now look at the word *rectifier*. This word means "*one* who puts right/corrects." See the associations parallel of the time of Noah's ark and the flood? Now as far as the word *mercury* goes, I will just say for now the planet Mercury is associated with trace amounts of aluminum, but it is also associated with the chemical element, the ancient deity Hermes who holds the caduceus, and, of course, the mercury used in this device, mercury-arc rectifier. Additionally, the caduceus is associated with Mercury and is the symbol of the practice of medicine.

If you look at this device, you will see that the main compo-nents are named as such: arms, neck, and head of the unit. At the end of each arm is a component that has similar characteristics to a cellular phone and is adjacent to the head of the unit, similar to how you would hold a cellular phone to your head. Another profound feature about this device is that its initial design was created with six (6) arms, six (6) diodes, and six (6) anodes. Its final design and development resulted in six (6) diodes with one (1) unit and six (6) anodes, and if you read papyrus 115, the most ancient text, you will learn that this was another number of the beast: 616.

Moving on, the next important, revealing characteristic of this "device" is its measured electrical properties. It is measured as a 600-volt three-phase system. Realize that *phase* also means gain and *gain* means score. Thus, you have 600-volt three scores with six arms, so six hundred threescore and six—again, another way the mark is calculated.

The way this device works is that it has to be excited/activated, and this can be done simply by radio signals/frequency. When this is done, the mercury becomes vaporous and moves from the neck of the unit into the head of the unit. This process is called excitation. At this stage, it becomes a *keep-alive circuit*. Knowing this, I would like to point out Revelation 9:6, "And in those days, men shall seek death, and shall not find it; and shall desire to die, and death shall flee from them."

Considering that, what if a device such as this could be placed in or on us and would keep us alive even if we want to die as Scripture alludes to? Now I want you to realize that this was technology developed over one hundred years ago. Our current technology has exponentially multiplied many times since this development. Remember, this device was the very beginning of radio, telecommunications that used RFID (radio-frequency identification). It helped birth radio, television, and walkie-talkies that have now evolved into our current cellular phone technology. I reiterate something this significant that was the beginning of today's technology should be widely taught and recognized, and yet it is not. You have to truly ask yourself, "Why?" It's my deduction that the principalities spoken of in Ephesians 6:12 (KJV) don't want you to see the end result and ultimate goal. If you lack knowledge, then you're more likely to accept a mark or commit idolatry as warned of in Scripture.

CHAPTER 2

MARK IN THE RIGHT HAND

S o now that this device has evolved into cellular phone technology, let's look at the main component of that name: *cellular*. It was given this name because its design function is made up and created similar to the human cell, hence the name *cell/cellular phone*. This alone should have drawn some concern or at least raised eyebrows, and yet it didn't. I say it is due to this programmed conditioning, slowly integrating this technology as a *device* to make our lives better. Now let's analyze another word associated: *handheld*. It clearly states in Scripture that one of the marks would be in the right hand. See that most people hold their cellular phones in their right hand and up to their head. Just like the design of the mercury-arc rectifier. Also, look at the word *device*, a two-syllable word of Latin origins meaning "of (de-) immoral or wicked behavior (-vice)." There is a specific piece of scripture warning of these "devices" in 2 Corinthians 2:11 (emphasis added), "Lest Satan should get an advantage of us, for we are not ignorant of his *devices!*" With that understood, there have been many that have noticed the bite out of the apple symbol used on the iPhone. This is a very clear association to the story of Adam and Eve and the *serpent in the tree* tricking them into eating of the tree they were told not to, thus committing the first sin. If the mark was just the iPhone, then most people would have to have them, and that's not the case. Therefore, it cannot be iPhone. Also, it's widely accepted that the mark would be an RFID chip. This is accurate to some degree, but again, there has been much speculation on this but very little solid evidence that lines up with Scripture until now. What I will reveal in depth. It is also speculated that it has to do with 5G technology. This idea is a distraction from the truth, a lie to have you looking for certain things while Lucifer is already implementing the mark. Think of it like a magician's trick, distracting you to look in one direction while the trick is actually playing out in the other hand. Much of the misdirection was disseminated because some people began to put things together, so the false propaganda campaign began and created much confusion.

Now many people think the mark is coming and is the RDIF *chip*, but isn't here yet. What if I told you it's already here and already in people's right hand but just hasn't been activated/excited like what has to be done with the mercury-arc rectifier? Your smartphones contain an RDIF chip. More specifically, the Bluetooth technology that is in every handheld cellular device.

Before I go further, I want to first cover the Bluetooth symbol itself. It is the most revealing aspect. Before I do, I want to reiterate the passage I pointed out earlier. Isaiah 46:9–10. Remember the ancient things. The most ancient thing is the story of mankind's beginning when God made the earth, mankind, and the garden of Eden and placed Adam and Eve in that garden. The story is told that they were told by God they could eat of every tree except the tree of knowledge of good and evil. But at some point, a *serpent entered into that tree* and convinced Eve to eat its fruit. This ultimately became man's first sin and fall from grace. Knowing this extremely important story of our beginnings, we would obviously need to be watchful and avoid at all cost any *serpents in trees*!

The *mark of the beast* in the hand is the same as the Bluetooth symbol located in *all* cell phones. It was created by using this symbol: ⵌ, which is an ancient rune/symbol for *serpent*. Then they used this symbol: ᛒ, which is the ancient rune/symbol for tree and birth. They then took the serpent symbol and placed it inside the symbol of the tree. Hence, the Bluetooth symbol means "the serpent in the tree and its birth" from its pre-Viking era. Ergo, "mark of the beast" in the right hand is you holding your cellular phone *device* in your hand, for most people, the right hand, just as Scripture warned the mark will be in.

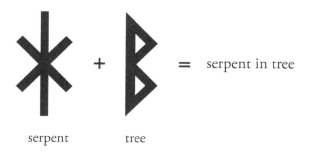

serpent   tree

You might say in considering this, it says the mark will be 666. Let's evaluate the symbol and see if it also is 666. Note that ancient runes were written using straight lines and sharp angles. Their 6 would be a straight line with a sharp angle as opposed to the curvature like our 6.

There is the 666! Three sixes within one symbol.

If that still isn't enough to convince you, then let's go to another test in Scripture. Revelation 13:15 says, "And he had power to give life unto the beast, that the image of the beast should both speak and cause that as many as would not worship the image of the beast should be killed." It's no secret that most people practically worship their phones, which is idolatry according to Scripture. The worst punishment you can give a child or even an adult nowadays is to take away their phone. See that Lucifer will use man's own *devices* against him just as Scripture states. Also, realize that your phone can also speak to you just as that piece of scripture warns of in Revelation 13:2–5. The dragon gave the beast the power to speak. The computer language that has evolved into the technology that allows your phones to speak back to you came from the first computer language called DRAKON, which is the ancient word for *dragon!* Just further proof.

And if there is still yet any doubt, let's look at the phrase *image of the beast*. The word *image* has two syllables. IM means instant memory, then AGE. Now test that with Scripture. This concept can be compared with Daniel 12:4 as it also relates to end-time prophecy: "Men will run to and fro, and knowledge shall be increased." Cellular phones have allowed this prophetic scripture to be fulfilled because we can get almost any knowledge from our cell phones at any time. Now you might ask, "What is the beast?" We know that one of the beasts of Revelation has two horns, that it would be some animal-type creature, and that it would need to be associated with the internal memory of your phone. What could it be, then? RAM (random access memory). The acronym is RAM. A ram is a two-horned beast, and the ancient deity worshiped by the Egyptians was *Re*: part ram, part man. This deity we know today is called Baphomet, and his association with *Satan* is well known.

One last piece of compelling proof I would like to share and provide from Scripture is Matthew 24:37: "But as the days of Noah were, so shall also the coming of the son of man be." This scripture states whatever was the problem in Noah's day that led God to send the flood to cleanse the earth would be again in the end when Christ returns. Look to Genesis 6:4, and you can also go to another Hebraic manuscript called *The Book of Giants* to find the answer.

The aspect from this was also revealed to me by the Lord. The giants of Noah's time as it parallels our time are giants of the industry. The tech giants are the Nephilim of our times; they have created these devices that consume and corrupt us today just as the giants of Noah's time corrupted and consumed mankind. In knowing this, you cannot also forget the banking giants. They also are the most important of all because everything needs money and financing to become a giant of the industry. We have also all heard the old saying that money is the root of *all* evil. It's more true than most realize. It is another form of idolatry, and the symbol of money is a serpent and a rod, which will become more relevant in later chapters. But note that this *mark* cannot be implemented until a given time. You will know when that time comes, and you will have to make a decision to either accept it or put down your cellular phones. Remember what the scriptures say in Revelation 13:17. You will not be able to buy or sell without the mark, and notice that all the payment methods are moving toward using your cell phones to pay for and make purchases with. But not only that, they are making these apps for the phones to track COVID-19 infections and vaccine passports via Bluetooth technology also. The serpent in the tree. Satan's trade*mark*!

CHAPTER 3

MARK IN THE FOREHEAD

I was one of the first to teach this when COVID-19 first occurred and can prove I published before these others who just saw what I was revealing and how accurate I was. I said this virus would span the globe before it did in accordance with Revelation and showed its association to Scripture. When everyone saw just how accurate I was and that I had prophesied beforehand events that came to pass, many began just following what I was revealing. They were only imitating what I had already revealed in published and time-stamped videos on social media. What I revealed in those videos and am reiterating now is that the evil powers that be would use this *pandemic* to implement the *mark* of the beast in the forehead and hand. When people saw that everything I was revealing was coming to pass, they began to spread the message because I was showing that we were in those times, and now over a year later, you see just how big this movement has become. But I can without question prove I was the first to reveal all of this through time-stamped videos.

The first warning from God about vaccines came with the smallpox vaccine. This vaccine from many decades ago left a *mark* in the arm of every person who received it. At this point, everyone should have taken notice, but they didn't. That ancient serpent did exactly with this as he did with the cell phone and other technology. Used it as a good thing to conditionally program people to accept it willingly just as warned of in scriptures. I want to first reveal what is in today's common flu vaccine and test it with Scripture. The first I want to explain is aluminum *salt*. Go to Matthew 5:13 (emphasis added): "You are the *salt* of the earth. But if the salt loses its saltiness, how can it be made salty again? It is no longer good for anything." In analyzing this, see that they are putting a different salt in us by means of the vaccines, aluminum salts, thus, making our salts from God no good for anything, just as Scripture says. There is another element to this I'd also like to point out. Aluminum is a commonly used conductor of electricity, and our brains do have an electrical response called synaptic firing. It's been shown in studies that the aluminum from these vaccines makes its way into our brains and creates plaque and other problems that disrupt this firing and has been attributed to Alzheimer's and autism. Also, notice the vaccine seems to be creating blood clots in the brains of some that take it, proving this goes into the brain. This unequivocally shows these salts that are mentioned and warned of in the Bible and the idea that we are the salt, which can be physically observed from the fact that our sweat tastes salty and when we sweat too much and lose too much salt too quickly, our body cramps.

Now look at another element in these vaccines, thimerosal. Notice this word is used to mask the fact that this is actually organic *mercury*. This one is extremely important because it goes back to being directly related to the *mercury-arc rectifier* that I revealed was the beginning of all this technology to the cellular phones, but see how it relates to vaccines also because this gets that mercury in your body that when excited, goes into your head just like the rectifier. This mercury can be measured or excited by any radio frequency device as long as it is the right frequency. I argue this has been well put in place: in the stores with the scanners that check the bar codes, the scanners you walk through at the store doors, and more revealing are the temperature scanners that can measure your temperature—those they put to your foreheads. Note this also puts numbers on your forehead just as warned of in Scripture, and if this is done using Bluetooth technology, then it is 666 on your forehead, as I've shown previously. This was that warning to us of what was occurring, the times we were in, and what I revealed that helped everyone see that the store scanners and thermostats are quite similar and in place at almost every retail outlet. They can be used to measure and excite mercury and aluminum (Revelation 13:17).

There are many factors to this element of vaccines. The most obvious is we all know that mercury is poisonous, so consider why it is added. Also, mercury is highly conductive, which can inhibit our synaptic firing and brain function just as aluminum does. One important aspect is that mercury is directly related to the caduceus, which is the symbol of the practice of medicine. That is an entire book in itself, but understand that just like in the times of Noah, we will be in the end and that are giants. Realize that the parallel of today's times is the pharmaceutical giants that control these vaccines. One more important scripture proof I'd like to show is Revelation 9:6: "Men will seek death and will not find it." Remember, I showed that one of the mercury-arc rectifier's other names was the keep-alive circuit! Once this is *excited* via RFID like the mercury-arc rectifier that is being put into us via vaccines and cellular phone technology, it will keep us alive even when we wish to die. Some of the other misdirection, confusion, and lack of knowledge is about this RFID chip. I've already shown that the Bluetooth in your phone is RFID, but how could a chip be in your forehead? One word: *nanotechnology*. The tech giants of our time that parallel the giants of the time of Noah have been hard at work, and just like I've pointed out before, Lucifer has a misinformation campaign to have you looking for a chip you can visibly see. I'd like to point out what Jesus taught the apostles in Matthew 13:13, "Our eyes see without seeing and ears hear without hearing." You cannot see or hear radio frequency. Also, you cannot see nanotechnology, and this is exactly where our technology is today. A microchip is literally the size of a virus, hence *coronavirus*. You cannot see nanotechnology; it is so small. And that is exactly how advanced today's technology is. There's much more scripture proof on that, but I feel certain this is ample proof on that to move on to the next element.

Egg proteins are a third element of the vaccines. Vaccines are created by injecting the virus into bird eggs and allowed to mutate to create a vaccine, supposedly the major component. Understand that when you inject animal proteins into your body, it mingles with your own DNA because proteins are DNA. The scripture that warns of this is Ecclesiastes 3:21. This DNA mingling can keep your spirit from going up just as that passage warns of. This also changes you on a cellular level, so consider also cellular phones and the synonymous relationship. See that this is clearly warned of in the Bible. Another aspect of this is now that these vaccines animal proteins are in our bodies, we now are susceptible to viruses that only animals used to get. Now we see increases in viruses such as SARS, MERS, swine flu, bird flu, and now COVID-19, a direct result because we are now susceptible to what scientists call zoological disease derived from animals. These are especially bad because unlike animals, our bodies are not meant to fight off these new diseases, leading to higher infection and mortality rates.

Before I go any further, I want to touch on some scriptures I believe to be extremely important as it relates to the medical field and the symbolism thereof. Note that many places in Scripture warns to be wary of serpents. One passage that can be found is Matthew 10:16. It states, "Be wise as serpents", but can also be translated to "be wary of." In knowing this, wouldn't it be very clear to look out for serpents as a basic, common-sense understanding? Knowing this, I'd like to point out it's been right in front of everyone's eyes all along, but just like with the cell phone, you have been programmed to believe it's good and just science. With the cellular phone, they sort of hide the symbol of the serpent using ancient runes, but Scripture still applies as I pointed out in Isaiah 46:9–10. Let's first look at the caduceus:

Clearly a rod with two serpents coiled around it constricting the staff. I want to point out Psalm 23:4: "His rod and staff they comfort me." Again, the warning of serpents, but it is more important to see the spiteful nature of the serpent. His nature is to defile, twist, and be blasphemous against God by putting his *mark*, constricting God's rod as mentioned in Psalm 23:4. You might argue this is still only Greek mythology, but let me reveal that the caduceus was the staff of Hermes and Hermes was the son of Maia, "the eldest of the seven sisters of the Pleiades." They are mentioned in the Bible as I've shown in Job 9:9 and Job 38:31. So clearly, whether you choose to see this symbolically or spiritually, this is not a good thing because God tells Job that he bound the Pleiades for some reason. If he bound the mother of Hermes, it could be possible Hermes holds ill will toward God, and this is verified by his staff having two serpents on it. It is symbolic that he teamed up with not just one but two serpents. This is not a good sign, and yet it is the symbol of the practice of medicine, which is also called sorcery in the Bible. The use of unnatural chemicals or animal proteins injected into our bodies. I want you to understand at this point that the caduceus evolved from something even more ancient, a rod that was more revealing and relevant.

Just as a brief mention, look at the Bowl of Hygeia, which is the symbol for pharmacy/*pharmakeia* as mentioned in Galatians 5:19–20 and is referred to as witchcraft/sorcery. Notice that this symbol once again depicts a serpent, and this time, it's constricting the Holy Grail, spitting its poison into it. With that being revealed, let me show scriptures that makes thi significant and show how blasphemous this symbol is against Jesus Christ (1 John 1:7, Matthew 26:26–28). What makes Hygeia relevant is that she is the daughter of Asclepius. See that all these spirits are all in plain sight and in our daily lives at this very time.

Now to the most significant symbol: the Rod of Asclepius. Notice again the serpent and the rod; this could also be depicted as the *serpent in the tree*, just like the Bluetooth symbol.

This is where it begins to all fall into place and come together in these times. The Rod of Asclepius was the first symbol of medicine in ancient times. Asclepius was the son of Apollyon, which is just the Greek name for Abaddon and who is also known as Perdition as mentioned in Revelation 9:11. If you read Scripture, you will see that Abaddon is the king of the pit. He is released on earth, bringing plagues and suffering upon the earth in the end times. With that said, also note that Asclepius's mother's name was Princess Coronis, which is just the plural form of *corona* as like *coronavirus*. And just like Hermes, consider if God imprisoned Abaddon, Asclepius's father, in the pit. You would think he would have a grudge, hence, the partnership of his staff with a serpent around it. He also teamed up with the serpent who is *Satan*.

Let's now take a look at the mother of Asclepius. You might still argue that this is still simply Greek mythology. His mother, Princess Coronis, was the princess of the Thessalonians; and you can find her son, "son of Perdition" mentioned in the book of Thessalonians, which I will reveal soon. What's most important is his mother Princess Coronis. *Coronis* is just the plural form of *corona*. Also important is the word *coronis*. It literally means "a mark at the end of a novel"! See that the powers that have named this virus the *novel coronavirus*!

See that the *mark of the beast* is implemented at the end of the Bible, which is a *novel* in literature terms, and her name as well as this virus named after her is one and the same. If that's not convincing enough, her name also means "curved one." See how much emphasis is being placed on "flattening the curve of infection"! Realize that important scripture, John 1:1 (emphasis added): "God is the *Word*, and the *Word* is with him." God is revealing through *the Word* what is unfolding before our very eyes because he is the *Word*, just as Scripture says.

What also extremely important in all of this is the fact that one of Abaddon's well-known other names is Perdition because he was sent into perdition, the pit for his transgressions against God. This is where the phrase "road to perdition" comes from. If you transgress against God, you follow the same road as him, *Abaddon*, and end up in the pit. Now it becomes relevant to these times. *Asclepius* is the son of Apollyon/Perdition/Abaddon, as specifically mentioned in 2 Thessalonians 2:3. I reiterate that Asclepius's mother was Princess Coronis of the Thessalonians and also why he is found in the book of Thessalonians. This provides more than enough proof that this deity is not just mythology. Biblical scripture ties Asclepius into the end-time events in this chapter specifically, as I've now proven. Now take a look at the very next verse "*Who* opposeth and exalteth himself above all that is called God, or that is worshiped; so that he as God sitteth in the temple of God shrewing himself that he is God" (2 Thessalonians 2:4; emphasis added). Many have always believed that this verse is a question but clearly see that it ends with a period, so it is not a question. The verse is naming *who*; that is a question that is its own answer. This idea is true, but see how this verse ends with a period? It's not a question in the literal sense but metaphorically a question that is its own answer. I reveal to you now that the "who" in this verse is WHO, the acronym for World Health Organization. See that their symbol is the Rod of Asclepius/son of Perdition exalted over the entire earth with the laurel wreath of victory, which is Apollyon/Abaddon's symbol exalted above and around the earth, all of God's creation, just as Scripture states would occur. The Rod of the son of

25

Perdition exalted of all of God's creation, proclaiming his victory just as stated in 2 Thessalonians 2:3–4.

 World Health Organization

This is their symbol; that is what was warned of from these passages. The reason this is significant is that the World Health Organization's main function and authority are to oversee and regulate all vaccination programs on the entire earth. To make sure as many people are vaccinated in accordance with their standards.

CHAPTER 4

THE TEMPLE

You might question now about WHO (World Health Organization) sitting in the temple of God and believe that this does not symbolize him being in God's temple because most have been led to believe that this temple of God is the temple in Jerusalem. The true location of this temple can be plainly found in Scripture, and it *is not* the temple located in Jerusalem. This was a misinformation campaign by Satan so that people would be waiting for that temple to be rebuilt and the antichrist to enter into it.

Go to 1 Corinthians 3:16. This verse very specifically tells you what the temple is. This verse specifically states that *you/we* are the temple. If you still need further proof, go to John 2:19 where even Jesus refers to his body being the temple. If Jesus Christ says the body is the temple, then it obviously is. If that still isn't enough proof, then realize that you have what is called a temporal lobe in your *forehead*, and this is exactly where *the mark of the beast* is: *in the forehead*. It is said to be put on in accordance with Revelation 7:13. See again God's warning to seal up your foreheads. Notice these forehead-scanning, temperature-measuring devices that only now with this pandemic have been completely adopted. They put a number *mark* on your forehead just as warned in Scripture. I revealed this first and can absolutely prove it with time-stamped videos, and it was only after I revealed this that everyone realized how accurate it was in accordance with Scripture.

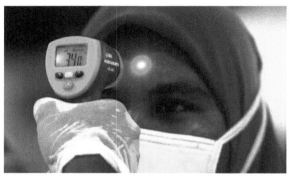

How and when the mark is implemented

This is the most important aspect of the *mark*. Just like the mercury-arc rectifier, the *mark* will have to be *excited*, and this can be done with the Bluetooth RFID chip in your cell phones, or the scanners in the stores, or by these temperature scanners using that same Bluetooth RFID. These scanners can also measure if you have had the vaccine by measuring the mercury and aluminum your head that is injected via the vaccines so that if you don't have the vaccine, you won't be allowed to buy or sell, just as what the policies that are being pushed in these times dictate. Just like the COVID-19 vaccination passports and the tracking by means of your phones and Bluetooth they are trying to implement that I also prophesied would happen at the very beginning of this pandemic. As of right now, because I revealed all these events in social media before they even occurred and because many saw my prophecy and saw how accurate it was and began to spread the message, the plan of these evil powers didn't work out as well as they expected. If (and that is a major *if* at this point simply because I did expose it) these powers that be cannot achieve what's called herd immunity, then they will have to simply abandon this plan to implement the *mark of the* beast, and consider that me prophesying these events before they even occurred helped people to be aware. Their plan will likely fail. But if they achieve that goal of getting so many vaccinated proportionate to the population, then they can implement the *mark*. Thanks to the Lord giving me these divine revelations before these events actually occurred, I was able to prophesy on his behalf and warn the world, and because my prophecy went viral on social media, I believe these evil principalities will be thwarted and God's omnipotence and power have ruled these times and won this battle. *All praise and glory be with him and the Savior Jesus Christ!*

As a bonus, I want to reveal a secret that one of the most powerful and influential leaders in the world has: Nancy Pelosi, the Speaker of the House that controls all legislation, including the laws regarding the COVID-19 laws and the purse strings and financial state of America. Her maiden name is D'Alessandro, but that was not her original family name. Her original family name was D'Medici, which means "family of medicine." Her ancestors changed this after they were expelled from Italy in the late 1400s after they bankrupted Italy because they controlled the purse strings in that time for their sorcery/practice of medicine. Now with that, remember what Ecclesiastes 1:9 teaches: "That which has been will be again, there is no new thing under the sun." See that the same events seem to be unfolding in America as she controls the laws with finance and medicine/*COVID-19 vaccine.*

About the Author

Kenneth Spears is an American Christian writer from Louisiana. He was raised in a good Christian home that understood the importance of biblical study. Before even attending grade school, his mother and stepfather, who were also both teachers, would take the time to read Scripture every evening and teach him discernment of the Word of God. This, he believes, was the most important part of his development as a child. His grandfather who he is named after was also a deacon at a small community church, and he too played a major role in establishing a moral compass within him using a biblical foundation. This was taught because no matter what happens in your life, if a child's foundation is built on Christ and the holy Word of God, then no matter what trials that person goes through, they will always be able to weather the storm.

Ken has spent years studying the Bible and researching in depth the earlier editions of it. Bible stories are history that changes views with every decade. After years of traveling, one can see just how sites change through construction and religious wars. But his greatest interest is nature, like exploring the forest land and all of God's beautiful creations, where he can speak to God in the quiet places he made on earth. Serenity fuels many religious thoughts for discussion. Ken confirms his arguments with Bible scriptures to prove certainty. Before writing this book, he continuously made YouTube videos of his religious views, opinions, and prophecies. If you want to know when Ken's next book will be released, please visit his publisher's website at http://www.christianfaithpublishing.com.

CPSIA information can be obtained
at www.ICGtesting.com
Printed in the USA
BVHW090214211221
624507BV00020B/725